THE
FAT
BURNER
Smoothies

Fat Burning Smoothie Recipes for Weight Loss, Cleanse and Optimal Health

DIANE SHARPE

Vineyard Press

Contact:
dianesharpe@weightlosspeeps.com

ISBN-13: 978-1494983086
ISBN-10: 1494983087

Printed in the United States of America

TABLE OF CONTENTS

INTRODUCTION 1

USING THE POWER OF FAT BURNING INGREDIENTS 3

HOW TO GET THE MOST FROM EVERY GLASS 7

MORNING FAT BURNER SMOOTHIES 9

Mango Chia Punch Smoothie...9

Berry Pine Smoothie.. 11

Pear Pleasure Smoothie 12

Spiced Oats Smoothie.. 13

Peachy Oats Smoothie... 14

Blissful Banana Smoothie 15

Amazing Cantaloupe Smoothie 16

Sizzling Strawberry Smoothie 17

Coffee Delight Smoothie.. 18

Almond Mint Smoothie.. 19

Banana Power Smoothie.. 20

Orangey Date Smoothie... 21

Cina-berry Smoothie 22

Almond Butter Smoothie 23

Raspberry Banana Smoothie... 24

Pumpkin Energy Smoothie 25

Kiwi Sunrise Smoothie.. 26

Orangey Papaya Smoothie... 27

Old Banana Oats Smoothie.. 28

GREEN FAT BURNER SMOOTHIES...29

Spinach Twist Smoothie...29

Liver Cleansing Smoothie..31

Strawberry Prize Smoothie..32

Hearty Kale Smoothie 33

Blackberry Paradise Smoothie 34

Cucumber Cooler Smoothie...35

Lettuce Treat Smoothie 36

Banana Blues Smoothie..37

Apricot Secret Smoothie 38

Oh Celery Smoothie..39

Mango Green Smoothie 40

It's Really Green Smoothie 41

Mango Vibes Smoothie 42

Green Pear Smoothie..43

Celeberry Smoothie 44

Tropical Mood Smoothie..45

EVERYDAY FAT BURNER SMOOTHIES **47**

Acai Berry Smoothie...47

Calorie-Down Smoothie 49

Mango Medley Smoothie..50

Power-Up Smoothie..51

Berry Pleaser Smoothie..52

Watermelon Ginger Smoothie 53

Chia Plum Delight Smoothie..54

Avocado Ginger Smoothie..55

Mixed Berries Smoothie...56

Super Energy Smoothie..57

Flax Berry Smoothie...58

Sweet Potato Dessert Smoothie 59

Healthy Watermelon Smoothie 60

Kiwi Apple Smoothie 61

Tropical Kiwi Smoothie 62

Blue Vanilla Smoothie 63

Simple Raspberry Smoothie 64

Summer Berry Smoothie 65

Cherry Almond Smoothie 66

Red Dream Smoothie 67

Coco Green Smoothie 68

Raspberry Blend Smoothie 69

Low Calorie Cantaloupe Smoothie 70

Cherry Bliss Smoothie 71

CONCLUSION **73**

DISCLAIMER

The information provided in this book is for educational purposes only. I am not a physician and this is not to be taken as medical advice or a recommendation to stop eating other foods. The book is based on my experiences and interpretations of the past and current research available. You should consult your physician to ensure that the recipes in this book are appropriate for your individual circumstances. If you have any health issues or pre-existing conditions, please consult your doctor before implementing any of the information that is presented in this book. Results may vary from individual to individual. This book is for informational purposes only and the author does not accept any responsibilities for any liabilities or damages, real or perceived, resulting from the use of this information.

1

INTRODUCTION

IT'S A PLEASURE TO SHARE these fat burner smoothie recipes with you. I am confident that they will transform your health as it did mine. There's so much satisfaction in drinking a glass of simple ingredients and natural foods without worrying about weight gain, the dangers of artificial foods, heavy carbs and loads of hidden sugar. These are the types of recipes you will find in this book – nothing less.

While these smoothie recipes contain only natural fruit sugars as sweetener, they are full of tasty flavors and are easy to prepare. These smoothies are a great way to ensure that you and your entire family get the required daily serving of fruits and veggies (5-9 servings of fruits and vegetables), while burning stubborn fat. Not everyone loves the same fruits or veggies, so be assured that you can freely tweak these recipes to suit your own taste.

Health Benefits of Fat Burner Smoothies in a Nutshell

With these fat burning smoothies you will be able to:
- Burn fat more effectively while you boost your metabolism
- Curb your appetite
- Lose Weight and increase energy levels
- Lessen bloating and water retention
- Boost the levels of your body's natural fat fighter
- Surge your body's insulin sensitivity
- Improve your overall health while decrease your risk of diseases such as cancer, heart disease and type 2 diabetes
- Have enhanced longevity

Why These Recipes Really Work?

Firstly, I am happy to say that they certainly worked for me and many others. One of the many reasons some people fail to lose weight is because of a clogged or inefficient liver. Moreover, studies have shown that a fatty liver affects more than 50% of adult Americans. When the liver is damaged by toxins or clogged in some way, the liver loses its natural ability to clear fats and toxins from your body and therefore becomes clogged with all sort of unhealthy stuff.

When the liver can't help to de-fat the body, fatty deposits build up around your body much easier. Fat is an excellent solvent, so toxins, free radicals and hormones all build up around your cells. When functioning normally the liver manufactures substances like antihistamines which are essential to the immune system. A healthy liver will also help in proper digestion and food absorption. Additionally, it helps direct the stores of carbohydrates and the release of glucose in the body. Now, a fatty liver depletes the whole immune system as it makes every effort to cope with excess toxins left in the blood and in your entire body.

Importantly, in order to maintain a toxin-free liver you should incorporate green leafy vegetables such as Garlic, Grapefruit, Bitter Gourd, Dandelion greens, Spinach, Mustard greens, Turmeric, Beets, Carrots, Avocados, Apples, Broccoli, Lemons, Limes, Chicory, Whole Grains among others into your diet. These will help to increase the creation and flow of bile, the substance that removes waste from the organs and blood. Thus, further helping the body to get rid of excess fat easier.

The smoothie recipes in this book will gradually cleanse, activate and restore your liver's ability to fight fat build up and restore your body's immunity while also enhancing weight loss. This is a simple yet natural approach that works wonders in losing weight.

Many health advocates recommend a natural liver cleanse before going on a health streak to ensure that the maximum benefits are attained. You can get the Liver Cleansing Smoothie in Chapter 5 of this book. Furthermore, by introducing these smoothies, especially the green smoothies, into your daily routine, you will give your body a nutritional boost that will aid in detoxing plus continue to help your body to cleanse itself naturally.

USING THE POWER OF FAT BURNING INGREDIENTS

IT IS TRUE THAT THE WORDS "fat burner" has been lightly tossed around and is sometimes nothing more than a pun. But, you can rest assured that this book provides smoothies that really burn fat. This is because I've made effort to ensure they are made up of only the best fat burning ingredients.

FAT BURNING INGREDIENTS

The ingredients in these fat burner smoothies are used in combinations that promote a healthy liver in your body and incredible weight loss. They will help to keep the liver clean and healthy by filtering most if not all of the bad stuff that heavily supports obesity in your body. Studies have shown that a healthy liver will always ensure a much better metabolism in your body, thereby increasing its ability to burn fat.

Here's what you need to know about some of these ingredients:

SMOOTHIE SWEETENERS

The problem that I've had with most so-called "fat burning smoothies" is that they DO NOT contain healthy sweeteners. Scientific studies have revealed that eating a diet high in refined sugar is a leading cause of obesity. Sugar is directly converted to fat by your body, and the more sugar you eat, the fatter you will be. Many people think that eating fatty food is the main cause of too much weight gain. But that is not true. Unhealthy sugars are one of the main things that make you fat. Research has also shown that other sweeteners such as honey, agave syrup, splenda and aspartame may all contribute to weight gain. With this in mind, I have ensured that these smoothies use the safest sweeteners to promote weight loss and burn fat faster.

Fruits

Yes, even though fruits also contain sugar (fructose), it is far better for our health than processed or refined sugars. This is why fruits are the main sweetener in most of these smoothie recipes. Moreover, bananas, berries and other fruits contain simple sugars for a quick energy boost plus complex carbohydrates which provide energy for hours. In this case, you won't experience the sugar crash that you get from artificial sugars or energy drinks. Additionally, berries could easily be regarded as the perfect weight-loss food. Berries have natural fructose sugar that satisfies your longing for sweets and enough fiber so your body absorbs fewer calories as you eat.

Dates

Dates are a perfect natural substitute for unhealthy sugars and this is why I've used pitted dates in some of these recipes. However, you may also consider substituting 1 teaspoon organic dates sugar for 1 pitted date.

What are the health benefits of dates? Dates are fruits and they are an extremely rich source of dietary fiber, vitamins and minerals. In addition, dates are also effective in improving cognitive functions, maintaining healthy blood pressure, enhancing immune system and relieving migraine, asthma and sore muscles. Even though dates provide more calories than most fruits, they make a great substitute for processed sweets, like candy, to help you stick to your weight-loss routine. Furthermore, the high fiber content in dates facilitates weight loss because they help fill you up faster and keep you feeling full longer.

Where to buy dates? I buy my dates from Amazon because it's so convenient.

SMOOTHIE BASE:

By adding a liquid base (or fruits with high liquidity in some cases) in smoothies it allows the solid ingredients to move around in your blender to get the right thickness and consistency.

Water or Ice?

You'll find this book suggesting pure filtered water or ice in some of these smoothie recipes. Water based smoothies are lower in calories, easier on your pockets and can be just as satisfying. Ice (made with pure filtered water) is also a great choice and usually it will give your smoothie an ideal and frothy consistency. Therefore, if you like your smoothie less icy then these smoothies will work just the same. Just add according to your taste or liking since water or ice will not really alter the amount of nutrients.

Furthermore, water contains zero calories and helps to boosts your metabolic rate, which in turn gives you energy and helps to burn more calories.

Unsweetened Almond Milk

In this book, I've used unsweetened almond milk as a liquid base for some recipes. Almond milk is one of the most nutritionally valuable milk substitutes available today. It is high in a number of vitamins and minerals, including vitamin E, manganese, magnesium, phosphorous, potassium, selenium, iron, fiber, zinc and calcium. Almond milk is low in calories, at only 40 calories per eight ounce serving, and low in fat. It contains only 3 grams of fat per eight ounce serving. Almond milk is lactose, gluten, casein and cholesterol free; it's also free of saturated fats. Consequently, almond milk is a beneficial addition to any diet geared towards weight loss or weight management. If you prefer to use dairy (for whatever reason), you may use your preferred fat-free milk. It is advised that you use other healthy substitutes which may include pure filtered water, coconut water, and coconut milk.

Juice

When it comes to juices, I like to keep it freshly squeezed. I would suggest that you stay away from the juices that contain high fructose corn syrup as these additives can negatively affect weight, blood sugar levels, digestion, among other health issues. Overall, you are not limited to what type of juice you can use – orange, apple, pineapple, cranberry, grape or others. It's your choice. My recommendation is to always choose organic options over others. If you can't get your juice freshly squeezed, you may opt for pure filtered water or coconut water.

Another great alternative is coconut water since it is naturally refreshing, sweet and has nutty taste. This is the clear liquid in the fruit's center that is tapped from young, green coconuts. It contains easily digested carbohydrate in the form of natural sugar and electrolytes. It is extremely good at hydrating the body and also helps with a number of conditions, from hangovers to cancer and kidney stones.

Note that an 11 ounce container has about 60 calories and if you drink several in one day, the calories will add up quickly. If you can get it, this may be another great option when adding liquid to some smoothies.

OTHER VITAL ADDITIVES:

Chia Seeds are a great source of fiber and can add thickness to your smoothie. It is a good idea to soak them a bit to soften them before adding them to your smoothie. The soluble fiber in Chia seeds helps to suppress hunger. In addition, the essential fatty acids contained in Chia seeds helps to boost metabolism and promote lean muscle mass, which is crucial for weight loss.

Goji Berries are a great way to pack antioxidants into your smoothie that will give you an extra kick of energy. Studies have shown that Goji berries assist in weight loss, nourishes the liver and kidneys and rejuvenating mind and body.

Flax Seed Oil is high in omega 3 fatty acids. Just add a tablespoon of flax seed oil and you'll have had your healthy fats for the day. It is a good idea to soak them a bit to soften them before adding them to your smoothie. Flax seeds' weight loss benefits come from their high fiber content and their wealth of Omega-3 fatty acids.

SMOOTHIE SUBSTITUTES

These smoothies can be easily tweaked to suit your personal preferences and to bring your wildest imagination alive. Also, wherever smoothie recipes are for 2 servings, you may cut the recipe in half for 1 serving.

Here are some listed smoothie substitute ingredient suggestions:

- Substitute pure filtered water for: unsweetened almond milk or unsweetened coconut water
- Substitute mango for : papaya or pineapple
- Substitute banana for: avocado
- Substitute cantaloupe for: honeydew, papaya, apple or pear
- Substitute strawberries for: raspberries or cherries
- Substitute blueberries for blackberries
- Substitute kale for spinach

HOW TO GET THE MOST FROM EVERY GLASS

TO HELP YOU GET THE MOST benefits from drinking these smoothies and to avoid some typical mistakes, I'll share my personal guidelines:

1. To make my smoothie routine much easier, I usually make my smoothie shopping list a week earlier and I usually prepare my smoothie first thing in the morning in the amount that I usually consume in one day.

2. After pouring enough smoothie in a glass for my morning satisfaction I store the rest in my refrigerator. I will to shake it well when I am ready to drink it as separation of the juices and fiber in the fruit usually occur.

3. I sip my smoothie slowly. Sometimes I even put my smoothie in a coffee mug with a lid and carry it with me to the car or to my office. This is a cute way of minimizing any chance of spilling it and keeping it private.

4. I never drink my smoothies with a meal. Not even with a candy.

5. I don't eat anything approximately 35 minutes before or 35 minutes after I've finished my smoothie. This is to ensure that I get the most nutritional benefit out of my smoothie.

6. If I decide to add more ingredients to my smoothie, I try to keep it simple in order to maximize nutritional benefits and to keep it easy on my digestive system.

7. I stick to my favorite (yes, I have favorites) delicious smoothies so that I am always looking forward to the next one. Taste

8. appeals to everyone differently, so it is almost natural that you'll come up with your own favorite recipes.

9. Particularly for green smoothies, I always rotate the green leaves that I add to my smoothies. This is because almost all greens in the world contain minute amounts of alkaloids. Note that tiny quantities of alkaloids will not cause you any harm and may even strengthen your immune system. However, if you keep consuming kale, or spinach, or any other single green for many weeks without rotating it, eventually it is possible that the same type of alkaloids can accumulate in your body and cause unwanted symptoms. Please note that you don't have to rotate the fruit in your green smoothies, just rotate the greens.

10. I choose organic produce whenever I go shopping. This is most important because consuming organic food gives superior nutrition in comparison to conventionally grown produce.

11. I never over drink. Whenever I am full, that's the time I stop drinking.

HOW TO MAKE THE BEST SMOOTHIES

Even though these smoothies are quick and easy to make, here are 5 steps that will help you to make the best smoothies every time:

Step 1: Add the liquid in your blender first. It is best to use a little under what may be necessary and then add extra later rather than have too much liquid and try to even it out from there.

Step 2: Add all of the fruits and vegetables that you want to include in the smoothie.

Step 3: Add anything extra to the smoothie for added flavorings, added nutrition or to change the consistency. These are your smoothie additives

Step 4: Add whole or crushed ice to the smoothie to help get the consistency to what you like. Note that depending on whether you are using frozen or fresh veggies and fruits, you will need to add more or less ice.

Step 5: Blend all ingredients together to make your smoothie. Usually it is good to pulse the blender a little until things get fairly mixed up, and then let the blender liquefy everything until it is smooth and exactly the consistency you want. At this point add more ice to make it thicker and more liquid to make it thinner. Pour and enjoy.

MORNING FAT BURNER SMOOTHIES

HOW ABOUT STARTING YOUR DAY with one of these fat burning breakfast smoothies? As a daily routine, these breakfast smoothies provides a nutritious and fulfilling treat to keep you hydrated while also providing you with a feeling of well-being all day long. They are packed with energizing nutrients full of antioxidants, vitamins, minerals and also other fat burning ingredients.

Mango Chia Punch Smoothie
Serving: 1

- 1 ripe Mango - peeled, pitted, chopped
- 1 teaspoon Nutmeg
- 1 cup unsweetened Almond Milk (cold)
- 1 tablespoon Organic Chia Seeds (pre-soaked overnight)
- ¾ teaspoon Vanilla Extract
- 2 Ice Cubes
- Pinch of Salt (optional)

Directions:

Place all ingredients into your blender and process until a smooth consistency is achieved. Pour in your favorite smoothie glass and enjoy.

Berry Pine Smoothie
Servings: 1

- ¼ cup fresh Pineapple Juice
- ½ cup Blueberries

- 1 cup Raspberries
- ½ cup unsweetened Almond Milk

Directions:

Place all ingredients into your blender and process until a smooth consistency is achieved. Pour in your favorite smoothie glass and enjoy.

Pear Pleasure Smoothie
Serving: 1

- 1 ripe Bananas, sliced
- 2 Pears, peeled, cored and quartered

- 2 Pitted Dates (optional)
- 1½ cups unsweetened Almond Milk

Directions:

Place all ingredients into your blender and process until a smooth consistency is achieved. Pour in your favorite smoothie glass and enjoy.

Spiced Oats Smoothie
Serving: 2

- 1 ½ cup unsweetened Almond Milk
- 1 teaspoon Vanilla Extract
- ¼ cup Quick-cook Oats
- 1 tablespoon Ground Flaxseed
- 1 teaspoon Ground Cinnamon
- 1 small ripe Banana (frozen works best)
- 2 Pitted Dates

Directions:

Place all ingredients into your blender and process until a smooth consistency is achieved. Pour in your favorite smoothie glass and enjoy.

Peachy Oats Smoothie
Servings: 2

- 1 cup Water
- 1½ cups of unsweetened Almond Milk
- 3 tablespoons Rolled Oats
- 1 very Ripe Peach, pitted and chopped
- 2 Pitted Dates
- ¼ cup freshly squeezed Orange Juice

Directions:

In a saucepan, add the water and rolled oats and bring to a boil; then lower the heat and simmer for approximately 3 minutes.

Remove the cooked oats from the heat and allow it to cool.

Place the cooled oat mixture in your blender and process until smooth, and then add the remaining ingredients. Process until a smooth consistency is achieved. Pour in your favorite smoothie glass and enjoy.

Note: Feel free to use your preferred Protein Mix.

Blissful Banana Smoothie
Serving: 1

- 1 cup Frozen Organic Blueberries
- 1 Ripe Banana, sliced
- 1 cup unsweetened Almond Milk
- 1 tablespoon Organic Chia Seeds (pre-soaked overnight)

Directions:

In a blender, combine banana, blueberries, almond milk, chia seeds and blend on high speed until smooth. Serve in your favorite smoothie glass and enjoy.

Amazing Cantaloupe Smoothie
Servings: 1

- 1 cup Cantaloupe, peeled, pitted & chopped
- 1 cup unsweetened Almond Milk
- ½ teaspoon Lime or

Lemon, juiced
- 1 tablespoon Organic Chia Seeds (pre-soaked overnight)

Directions:

Place all ingredients into your blender and process until a smooth consistency is achieved. Pour in your favorite smoothie glass and enjoy.

Sizzling Strawberry Smoothie
Serving: 1

- ½ cup fresh Strawberries
- ¼ cup freshly squeezed Orange Juice
- ½ cup unsweetened Almond Milk
- 1 tablespoon Organic Chia Seeds (pre-soaked overnight)
- 2 pitted Dates

Directions:

Place all ingredients into your blender and process until a smooth consistency is achieved. Pour in your favorite smoothie glass and enjoy.

Coffee Delight Smoothie
Serving: 2

- 1 cup unsweetened Almond Milk
- ¾ cup freshly brewed and cooled Black Coffee (use your favorite coffee - decaf or regular)
- 2 ripe Bananas, sliced
- 1 cup Ice Cubes

Directions:

Place all ingredients into your blender and process until a smooth consistency is achieved. Pour in your favorite smoothie glass and enjoy.

Almond Mint Smoothie
Serving: 2

- 1 teaspoon Nutmeg
- 1 teaspoon Vanilla Extract
- 2 pitted Dates
- ¼ cup Ground Almonds
- 2 Ripe Bananas (frozen works best)
- ¼ cup brewed and chilled Mint tea
- ¾ cup unsweetened Almond Milk
- 3-4 Ice Cubes

Directions:

Place all ingredients into your blender and process until a smooth consistency is achieved. Pour in your favorite smoothie glass and enjoy.

Banana Power Smoothie
Servings: 2

- 1 medium ripe Banana, frozen and sliced
- ¾ cup unsweetened Almond Milk
- 1 teaspoon Flax Seed Powder (or pre-soak flaxseeds)
- 1 tablespoon Organic Chia Seeds (pre-soaked overnight)
- 2 Walnuts
- 5 cubes of ice

Directions:

Place all ingredients into your blender and process until a smooth consistency is achieved. Pour in your favorite smoothie glass and enjoy.

Orangey Date Smoothie
Servings: 1

- 5 dried Dates, pitted
- ½ cup fresh Pineapple Juice
- 1 cup unsweetened

Almond Milk
- 1 tablespoon Organic Chia Seeds (pre-soaked overnight)

Directions:

Place all ingredients into your blender and process until a smooth consistency is achieved. Pour in your favorite smoothie glass and enjoy.

Cina-berry Smoothie
Servings: 2

- 1 cup unsweetened Almond Milk
- ½ cup fresh Raspberries
- 1 ripe Mango, cut into chunks
- ¼ cup frozen Blueberries
- ¼ cup frozen Strawberries
- ½ cup Papaya, sliced, seeds removed and cut into chunks
- 1 ripe Banana, sliced
- ½ large Carrot, sliced thinly
- 1 teaspoon of Cinnamon

Directions:

Place all ingredients into your blender and process until a smooth consistency is achieved. Pour in your favorite smoothie glass and enjoy.

Almond Butter Smoothie
Serving: 1

- 1 cup unsweetened Almond Milk
- ½ ripe Banana, sliced
- 1 tablespoon Almond Butter (use homemade or without additives)
- 2 pitted Dates (optional)
- 4 Ice Cubes

Directions:

Place milk, banana, almond butter and dates into your blender and process until smooth. Add ice cubes and pulse. Pour in your favorite smoothie glass and serve.

Raspberry Banana Smoothie
Servings: 2

- 1 cup frozen Raspberries
- 1 Ripe Banana (frozen & sliced)

- 1 cup of unsweetened Almond Milk

Directions:

Place all ingredients into your blender and process until a smooth consistency is achieved. Pour in your favorite smoothie glass and enjoy.

Pumpkin Energy Smoothie
Serves: 2

- 1 cup unsweetened Almond Milk
- ¼ cup Rolled Whole Oats
- ¼ cup organic pureed Canned Pumpkin (or make your own pureed pumpkin)
- 1 tablespoon Chia Seeds, pre-soaked in water
- ½ frozen Ripe Banana
- 2 teaspoon Nutmeg
- 2 pitted Dates
- 3 Ice Cubes

Directions:

Place all ingredients into your blender and process until a smooth consistency is achieved. Pour in your favorite smoothie glass and enjoy.

Kiwi Sunrise Smoothie
Servings: 1-2

- 1 Ripe Banana, peeled and sliced
- 1 Kiwi Fruit, peeled and chopped
- 1 cup freshly squeezed Orange Juice

- ¼ cup freshly squeezed Grapefruit Juice
- ¼ cup fresh Pineapple Juice

Directions:

Place all ingredients into your blender and process until a smooth consistency is achieved. Pour in your favorite smoothie glass and enjoy.

Orangey Papaya Smoothie
Serving: 1

- ½ cup Orange Juice
- 1 cup unsweetened Almond Milk
- ½ of a medium Papaya - peeled, seeds removed and sliced
- ½ Ripe Banana, sliced
- 1 tablespoon Organic Chia Seeds (pre-soaked overnight) -optional
- 3 Ice Cubes

Directions:

Place all ingredients into your blender and process until a smooth consistency is achieved. Pour in your favorite smoothie glass and enjoy.

Old Banana Oats Smoothie
Serving: 1

- 1 cup unsweetened Almond Milk
- 1 ripe Banana, sliced
- ¼ cup Old-Fashioned Rolled Oats (uncooked)
- 2 pitted Dates
- 1 cup Ice Cups

Directions:

Place all ingredients into your blender and process until a smooth consistency is achieved. Pour in your favorite smoothie glass and enjoy.

GREEN FAT BURNER SMOOTHIES

THESE FAT BURNING GREEN smoothies are perfect to have any time of day and even for detox. These smoothies are also great for those who don't like the taste of bare veggies as well as for those who want to lose weight. A perfect combination to build a strong immunity against your fat genes. You will feel a renewed vitality through these specially prepared and fat burning green smoothies.

Spinach Twist Smoothie
Serving: 2

- 2 cups pure filtered Water
- ½ cup Strawberries
- ½ cup Raspberries
- 1 medium Mango, cut into chunks
- 1 cup Spinach, finely chopped

Directions:

Place all ingredients into your blender and process until a smooth consistency is achieved. Pour in your favorite smoothie glass and enjoy.

Liver Cleansing Smoothie
Serving: 3

- 1 cup spinach
- 3 artichoke hearts
- 1 green onion
- 2 celery stalks
- 2 cups purified water

Directions:

Place spinach, artichokes, onion, celery, and 1 cup of water in a blender and blend until thoroughly combined. Add remaining cup of water as needed while blending until desired consistency is achieved. Serve in your favorite smoothie glass and enjoy!

Note: Ideally, this should be taken in the morning, noonday and before bedtime, hence 3 servings. Usually, it works best when consumed without other meals. This may not be the best tasting smoothie or juice but it does the job very well. You should not take this as a continuous meal, just occasionally to flush out unhealthy stuff from the liver. You should also practice to avoid alcohol while drinking smoothies so that you get the full benefits. Studies have shown that alcohol is very bad for the liver.

Strawberry Prize Smoothie
Serving: 2

- 2 cups pure filtered Water
- 1 cup Strawberries
- 1 medium ripe Banana, sliced
- 1 cup Spinach, finely chopped
- 1 tablespoon Organic Chia Seeds (pre-soaked overnight)

Directions:

Place all ingredients into your blender and process until a smooth consistency is achieved. Pour in your favorite smoothie glass and enjoy.

Hearty Kale Smoothie
Serving: 2

- 1 cup Coconut Water
- 2 medium ripe Bananas

- 1 cup Kale, finely chopped

Directions:

Place all ingredients into your blender and process until a smooth consistency is achieved. Pour in your favorite smoothie glass and enjoy.

Blackberry Paradise Smoothie
Serving: 2

- 2 cups pure filtered Water
- ½ cup Blackberries
- ½ cup Cherries

- 1 medium ripe Banana
- 1 cup Pak Choi, finely chopped

Directions:

Place all ingredients into your blender and process until a smooth consistency is achieved. Pour in your favorite smoothie glass and enjoy.

Cucumber Cooler Smoothie
Serving: 1

- 1 cup pure filtered Water
- 2 Apples – peeled, cored, chopped
- 1 medium ripe Banana
- ½ Cucumber, chopped

Directions:

Place all ingredients into your blender and process until a smooth consistency is achieved. Pour in your favorite smoothie glass and enjoy.

Lettuce Treat Smoothie
Serving: 2

- 1 cup organic Coconut Water
- 1 cup Blueberries
- 1 medium ripe Banana, sliced
- 1 cup Romaine Lettuce, finely chopped

Directions:

Place all ingredients into your blender and process until a smooth consistency is achieved. Pour in your favorite smoothie glass and enjoy.

Banana Blues Smoothie
Servings: 2

- ½ medium ripe Banana, sliced
- ½ cup Blueberries
- 2 cups Spinach, finely chopped
- 1 large Orange, peeled and sliced
- 1/3 cup pure filtered Water
- 1 cup ice (optional based on preference)

Directions:

Place all ingredients into your blender and process until a smooth consistency is achieved. Pour in your favorite smoothie glass and enjoy.

Apricot Secret Smoothie
Serving: 2

- 2 cups pure filtered Water
- 1 cup Apricots
- 1 medium ripe Banana,

sliced
- 1 cup Kale, finely chopped

Directions:

Place all ingredients into your blender and process until a smooth consistency is achieved. Pour in your favorite smoothie glass and enjoy.

Oh Celery Smoothie
Serving: 1

- 1 cup pure filtered Water
- 3 Peaches, peeled, sliced
- 1 medium ripe Banana, sliced
- 1 Celery Stalk, finely chopped

Directions:

Place all ingredients into your blender and process until a smooth consistency is achieved. Pour in your favorite smoothie glass and enjoy.

Mango Green Smoothie
Serving: 2

- 2 cups pure filtered Water
- 1 cup Strawberries
- 1 Mango, cut into chunks
- 1 cup Romaine Lettuce, finely chopped

Directions:

Place all ingredients into your blender and process until a smooth consistency is achieved. Pour in your favorite smoothie glass and enjoy.

It's Really Green Smoothie
Serving: 2

- 1 cup Coconut Water (or pure filtered Water)
- 1 large ripe Mango, peeled, seed removed and cut into chunks (or use your favorite tropical fruit)
- ½ cup Kale, finely chopped
- 1 teaspoon Chia Seeds, pre-soaked in water
- 1 cup Parsley, finely chopped
- 1 stalk of Celery
- ½ cup Ice Cubes

Directions:

Place all ingredients into your blender and process until a smooth consistency is achieved. Pour in your favorite smoothie glass and enjoy.

Mango Vibes Smoothie
Serving: 2

- 2 cups pure filtered Water
- 2 ripe Mangoes, peeled, sliced and seeds removed
- 1 cup Pak Choi, finely chopped

Directions:

Place all ingredients into your blender and process until a smooth consistency is achieved. Pour in your favorite smoothie glass and enjoy.

Green Pear Smoothie
Serving: 2

- 2 cups pure filtered Water
- 2 Pears, peeled and sliced
- 1 medium ripe Banana, sliced
- ½ cup Spinach, finely chopped
- ½ cup Romaine Lettuce, finely chopped

Directions:

Place all ingredients into your blender and process until a smooth consistency is achieved. Pour in your favorite smoothie glass and enjoy.

Celeberry Smoothie
Serving: 2

- 2 Celery Stalks, finely chopped
- 1 cup Blueberries, fresh or frozen

- 11/2 cups unsweetened Almond Milk
- ½ cup of Ice

Directions:

Place all ingredients into your blender and process until a smooth consistency is achieved. Pour in your favorite smoothie glass and enjoy.

Tropical Mood Smoothie
Serving: 2

- 2 cups pure filtered Water
- ½ cup Pineapple, cut into chunks
- ½ cup Mango, cut into chunks
- 1 medium ripe Banana, sliced
- 1 cup Spinach, finely chopped

Directions:

Place all ingredients into your blender and process until a smooth consistency is achieved. Pour in your favorite smoothie glass and enjoy.

6

EVERYDAY FAT BURNER SMOOTHIES

THESE EVERYDAY FAT BURNING smoothies are made with superfoods that are extremely rich in nutrients and also really delicious. These will fight and guard you against obesity, heart disease, muscle loss, wrinkles, cancer, high blood pressure and other diseases. Boost your energy while you drink these highly nutritious smoothies and lose weight the natural way.

Acai Berry Smoothie
Serving: 2

- 1 cup fresh Acai Berry Juice
- 1 cup seedless Red Grapes
- 1 cup frozen Raspberries
- 1 cup unsweetened Almond Milk
- 1 tablespoon Organic Chia Seeds (pre-soaked)

Directions:

Place all ingredients into your blender and process until a smooth consistency is achieved. Pour in your favorite smoothie glass and enjoy.

Calorie-Down Smoothie
Servings: 2

- ½ cup unsweetened Almond Milk
- ½ medium ripe Banana, sliced

- 1 cup fresh Pak Choi, finely chopped
- 1 Kiwi, peeled and sliced

Directions:

Place all ingredients into your blender and process until a smooth consistency is achieved. Pour in your favorite smoothie glass and enjoy.

Mango Medley Smoothie
Serving: 2

- 2 cups Mangoes, diced (or frozen mango chunks)
- ½ cup Carrot Juice
- ½ cup Apple Juice
- ½ cup unsweetened Almond Milk
- ¼ teaspoon Cinnamon Powder
- ¼ teaspoon Grated Nutmeg
- ½ cup Ice Cubes (omit if using frozen mango chunks)
- ¼ teaspoon Vanilla Extract

Directions:

Place all ingredients into your blender and process until a smooth consistency is achieved. Pour in your favorite smoothie glass and enjoy.

Power-Up Smoothie
Serving: 2

- 1½ cup Unsweetened Almond Milk
- 2 small Ripe Bananas, peeled
- 1 tablespoon Cocoa Powder (or Fat-Free Chocolate Syrup)
- 1/3 cup Goji Berries, soaked
- 1 cup Red Grapes
- 2 cups (or large handfuls) of Fresh Baby Spinach - optional
- ½ cup Frozen Blueberries
- Water if needed

Directions:

In a blender, add the almond milk, followed by the bananas, red grapes, frozen blueberries, soaked goji berries, baby spinach, chocolate syrup or cocoa powder. Blend on high speed for about 30 seconds or until the smoothie is creamy smooth. Add a little water (or more fat-free milk) to suit your desired consistency. Pour in your favorite smoothie glass and enjoy.

Berry Pleaser Smoothie
Serving: 2

- 1½ cups Unsweetened Almond Milk
- 1½ tablespoons Cocoa Powder
- 1 teaspoon Cinnamon

- 1 ripe Banana, sliced
- ½ cup fresh or frozen Strawberries
- 2 pitted Dates

Directions:

Place all ingredients into your blender and process until a smooth consistency is achieved. Pour in your favorite smoothie glass and enjoy.

Watermelon Ginger Smoothie
Serving: 2

- ½ cup unsweetened Almond Milk
- 2 cups seeded Watermelon Chunks
- ½ teaspoon Ground Ginger
- 1 cup Ice Cubes
- 2 Pitted Dates (optional)

Directions:

Place all ingredients into your blender and process until a smooth consistency is achieved. Pour in your favorite smoothie glass and enjoy.

Chia Plum Delight Smoothie
Servings: 1

- 3 red Plums, halved & pitted
- 1 cup Unsweetened Almond Milk

- 1 tablespoon Organic Chia Seeds (pre-soaked for at least 1 hour)
- ¼ cup Ice Cubes

Directions:

Place all ingredients into your blender and process until a smooth consistency is achieved. Pour in your favorite smoothie glass and enjoy.

Avocado Ginger Smoothie
Serving: 1

- 1 whole Avocado, pitted and peeled
- 2 medium ripe Bananas, sliced
- ½ cup freshly squeezed Orange Juice
- ¼ cup unsweetened Almond Milk
- 1 tablespoon Ginger, grated
- 2 pitted Dates (optional)

Directions:

Place avocado, bananas, orange juice and almond milk into your blender and process until smooth. Add ginger and lime juice and blend until well combined and creamy. Pour in your favorite smoothie glass and serve.

Mixed Berries Smoothie
Serving: 2

- 1½ cups Unsweetened Almond Milk
- 2 cups fresh mixed Berries
- - use your favorite berries
- 1 tablespoon Flaxseed Oil
- ½ cup Ice Cubes

Directions:

Place all ingredients into your blender and process until a smooth consistency is achieved. Pour in your favorite smoothie glass and enjoy.

Super Energy Smoothie
Serving: 2

- 1 cup Unsweetened Almond Milk
- ½ frozen ripe Banana (large)
- 1 tablespoon Cocoa Powder
- 1 tablespoon Organic Chia Seeds (pre-soaked for at least an hour)
- 2 tablespoons Goji Berries
- 1 teaspoon Cinnamon
- 4 Ice Cubes

Directions:

Place all ingredients into your blender and process until a smooth consistency is achieved. Pour in your favorite smoothie glass and enjoy.

Flax Berry Smoothie
Serving: 2

- 1 tablespoon Ground Flaxseed
- ½ cup frozen Raspberries
- ½ cup frozen Blueberries
- 1 cup Unsweetened

Almond Milk
- 1 tablespoon Organic Chia Seeds (pre-soaked for at least an hour) - optional

Directions:

Place all ingredients into your blender and process until a smooth consistency is achieved. Pour in your favorite smoothie glass and enjoy.

Sweet Potato Dessert Smoothie
Serving: 1

- 1 cup Unsweetened Almond Milk
- ¾ cup Sweet Potato, cooked and chilled
- ½ cup ripe Bananas, frozen
- 1 teaspoon ground Cinnamon
- ¼ teaspoon Nutmeg

Directions:

Place almond milk in blender first, followed by bananas, sweet potatoes, cinnamon, and nutmeg. Blend until smooth. Pour into your favorite smoothie glass and serve.

Healthy Watermelon Smoothie
Serving: 2

- 2 cups Spinach
- 1½ cups Watermelon
- 1½ cups Cantaloupe
- ½ cup fresh Strawberries
- ½ cup fresh Raspberries
- ¼ cup Almond Milk
- ¾ cup Ice Cubes

Directions:

Place all ingredients into your blender and process until a smooth consistency is achieved. Pour in your favorite smoothie glass and enjoy.

Kiwi Apple Smoothie
Serving: 1

- 4 Kiwi, peeled and sliced
- 1 cup frozen Banana slices
- 1 cup fresh Apple Juice

- 1/2 cup frozen Strawberries

Directions:

Place all ingredients into your blender and process until a smooth consistency is achieved. Pour in your favorite smoothie glass and enjoy.

Tropical Kiwi Smoothie
Serving: 2

- 1 cup Blueberries
- ¼ large Pineapple, core removed and cubed
- 1 Kiwi Fruit, peeled and sliced

- 1 ripe Banana, sliced
- ½ Pear
- ½ cup pure filtered Water
- 4 Ice Cubes

Directions:

Place all ingredients into your blender and process until a smooth consistency is achieved. Pour in your favorite smoothie glass and enjoy.

Blue Vanilla Smoothie
Serving: 1

- 1 cup Unsweetened Almond Milk
- 2 teaspoon Vanilla Extract
- ½ cup frozen Blueberries
- 1 teaspoon Nutmeg, grated

Directions:

Place all ingredients into your blender and process until a smooth consistency is achieved. Pour in your favorite smoothie glass and enjoy.

Simple Raspberry Smoothie
Serving: 1

- 1 cup unsweetened Almond Milk

- ½ cup frozen Raspberries

Directions:

Place all ingredients into your blender and process until a smooth consistency is achieved. Pour in your favorite smoothie glass and enjoy.

Summer Berry Smoothie
Servings: 2

- ¼ cup organic Apple Juice
- ½ cup Red Apple, cored and sliced
- ¼ cup Blueberries

- ¼ cup Cranberries
- 1 teaspoon Ginger Root, grated

Directions:

Place all ingredients into your blender and process until a smooth consistency is achieved. Pour in your favorite smoothie glass and enjoy.

Cherry Almond Smoothie
Servings: 2

- 2 cups frozen Cherries
- 2 pitted Dates
- 1 cup unsweetened Almond Milk

- 1 tablespoon Organic Chia Seeds (pre-soaked for at least an hour) - optional

Directions:

Place all ingredients into your blender and process until a smooth consistency is achieved. Pour in your favorite smoothie glass and enjoy.

Red Dream Smoothie
Serving: 2

- ¼ cup Raspberries
- 5 large Strawberries, hulled
- ¼ cup fresh Cranberries

- 1 small Red Apple, cored
- 2 Pitted Dates
- 1¼ cups Unsweetened Almond Milk

Directions:

Place all ingredients into your blender and process until a smooth consistency is achieved. Pour in your favorite smoothie glass and enjoy.

Coco Green Smoothie
Servings: 2

- 6 large fresh Strawberries
- ½ medium Orange, peeled and sliced
- 1 medium ripe Banana, peeled and chopped
- 1½ cups Spinach
- ½ cup organic Coconut Water
- ¾ cup Ice

Directions:

Place the strawberries, orange slices, banana and spinach into a blender and process for about 30 seconds. Add the coconut water and ice and process once again until smooth. Pour into your favorite smoothie glass and serve.

Raspberry Blend Smoothie
Servings: 1

- 1 cup fresh or frozen Raspberries
- 1 Ripe Banana, peeled and chopped
- ¼ teaspoon Lemon Juice
- 1 cup unsweetened Almond Milk
- 1 tablespoon Organic Chia Seeds (pre-soaked for at least an hour)
- 2 Pitted Dates

Directions:

Place all ingredients into your blender and process until a smooth consistency is achieved. Pour in your favorite smoothie glass and enjoy.

Low Calorie Cantaloupe Smoothie
Serving: 2

- 1 medium ripe Cantaloupe, peeled, seeds removed and cut into chunks
- 1½ cup Unsweetened Almond Milk

- 1 tablespoon Organic Chia Seeds (pre-soaked for at least an hour)
- ¾ cup Crushed Ice
- 2 Pitted Dates (optional)

Directions:

Place all ingredients into your blender and process until a smooth consistency is achieved. Pour in your favorite smoothie glass and enjoy.

Cherry Bliss Smoothie
Serving: 2

- 1½ cups Frozen Cherries
- ¾ cup Frozen Blueberries
- 1 Ripe Banana, peeled
- 1 cup unsweetened Almond Milk
- 1 tablespoon Organic Chia
- Seeds (pre-soaked for at least an hour) - optional
- 4 Ice Cubes
- ¼ teaspoon Vanilla Extract
- 2 pitted Dates (optional)

Directions:

Place all ingredients into your blender and process until a smooth consistency is achieved. Pour in your favorite smoothie glass and enjoy.

7

CONCLUSION

I HAVE FOUND THESE RECIPES to be really beneficial to my overall health and I hope you will find much satisfaction as you explore all that this book has to offer. I invite you to freely leave a review of this book on Amazon. Also, if you wish to express any concerns you may email me at: dianesharpe@weightlosspeeps.com.

I truly value and appreciate your contribution in making my passion to improve the health of others around the world a reality. Good health is not a coincidence, it is a choice.

All the best,
Diane

Printed in Great Britain
by Amazon.co.uk, Ltd.,
Marston Gate.